let's cook

vegetarian pasta

Tom
Bridge

p

Contents

Spinach Gnocchi with Tomato & Basil Sauce

These gnocchi or small dumplings are made with potato and flavoured with spinach and nutmeg and served in a rich tomato sauce for an ideal light meal.

Serves 4

INGREDIENTS

450 g/1 lb baking potatoes
75 g/2³/4 oz spinach
1 tsp water
25 g/1 oz/3 tbsp butter or vegetarian
   margarine
1 small egg, beaten

150 g/5¹/2 oz/³/4 cup plain
   (all-purpose) flour
fresh basil sprigs, to garnish

TOMATO SAUCE:
1 tbsp olive oil
1 shallot, chopped

1 tbsp tomato purée (paste)
225 g/8 oz can chopped tomatoes
2 tbsp chopped basil
85 ml/3 fl oz/6 tbsp red wine
1 tsp caster (superfine) sugar
salt and pepper

1 Cook the potatoes in their skins in a pan of boiling salted water for 20 minutes. Drain well and press through a sieve into a bowl. Cook the spinach in 1 tsp water for 5 minutes until wilted. Drain and pat dry with paper towels. Chop and stir into the potatoes.

2 Add the butter or margarine, egg and half of the flour to the spinach mixture, mixing well.

Turn out on to a floured surface, gradually kneading in the remaining flour to form a soft dough. With floured hands, roll the dough into thin ropes and cut off 2 cm/³/4 inch pieces. Press the centre of each dumpling with your finger, drawing it towards you to curl the sides of the gnocchi. Cover and leave to chill.

3 Heat the oil for the sauce in a pan and sauté the chopped

shallots for 5 minutes. Add the tomato purée (paste), tomatoes, basil, red wine and sugar and season well. Bring to the boil and then simmer for 20 minutes.

4 Bring a pan of salted water to the boil and cook the gnocchi for 2–3 minutes or until they rise to the top of the pan. Drain well and transfer to serving dishes. Spoon the tomato sauce over the top. Garnish and serve.

Vegetable Pasta Nests

These large pasta nests look impressive when presented filled with grilled (broiled) mixed vegetables, and taste delicious.

Serves 4

INGREDIENTS

175 g/6 oz spaghetti
1 aubergine (eggplant), halved and sliced
1 courgette (zucchini), diced
1 red (bell) pepper, seeded and chopped diagonally

6 tbsp olive oil
2 garlic cloves, crushed
50 g/1³/₄ oz/4 tbsp butter or vegetarian margarine, melted
15 g/¹/₂ oz/1 tbsp dry white breadcrumbs

salt and pepper
fresh parsley sprigs, to garnish

1 Bring a large saucepan of water to the boil and cook the spaghetti until 'al dente' or according to the instructions on the packet. Drain well and set aside until required.

2 Place the aubergine (eggplant), courgette (zucchini) and (bell) pepper on a baking tray (cookie sheet).

3 Mix the oil and garlic together and pour over the vegetables, tossing to coat.

4 Cook under a preheated hot grill (broiler) for about 10 minutes, turning, until tender and lightly charred. Set aside and keep warm.

5 Divide the spaghetti among 4 lightly greased Yorkshire pudding tins (pans). Using a fork, curl the spaghetti to form nests.

6 Brush the pasta nests with melted butter or margarine and sprinkle with the breadcrumbs. Bake in a preheated oven, at 200°C/400°F/ Gas Mark 6, for 15 minutes or until lightly golden. Remove the pasta nests from the tins (pans) and transfer to serving plates. Divide the grilled (broiled) vegetables between the pasta nests, season and garnish.

COOK'S TIP

'Al dente' means 'to the bite' and describes cooked pasta that is not too soft, but still has a bite to it.

Marinated Aubergine (Eggplant) on a Bed of Linguine

This unusual, fruity marinade makes the aubergine (eggplant) slices simply melt in the mouth.

Serves 4

INGREDIENTS

150 ml/^{1}/$_4$ pint/^{5}/$_8$ cup
  vegetable stock
150 ml/^{1}/$_4$ pint/^{5}/$_8$ cup white
  wine vinegar
2 tsp balsamic vinegar
3 tbsp olive oil
fresh oregano sprig

450 g/1 lb aubergine (eggplant),
  peeled and thinly sliced
400 g/14 oz dried linguine

MARINADE:
2 tbsp extra virgin oil
2 garlic cloves, crushed

2 tbsp chopped fresh oregano
2 tbsp finely chopped
  roasted almonds
2 tbsp diced red (bell) pepper
2 tbsp lime juice
grated rind and juice of 1 orange
salt and pepper

1 Put the vegetable stock, wine vinegar and balsamic vinegar into a saucepan and bring to the boil over a low heat. Add 2 tsp of the olive oil and the sprig of oregano and simmer gently for about 1 minute.

2 Add the aubergine (eggplant) slices to the pan, remove from the heat and set aside for 10 minutes.

3 Meanwhile make the marinade. Combine the oil, garlic, fresh oregano, almonds, (bell) pepper, lime juice, orange rind and juice together in a large bowl and season to taste.

4 Carefully remove the aubergine (eggplant) from the saucepan with a slotted spoon, and drain well. Add the aubergine (eggplant) slices to the marinade,

mixing well, and set aside in the refrigerator for about 12 hours.

5 Bring a large pan of lightly salted water to the boil. Add half the remaining oil and the linguine and cook until just tender. Drain the pasta and toss with the remaining oil while still warm. Arrange the pasta on a serving plate with the aubergine (eggplant) slices and the marinade and serve.

Rotelle with Spicy Italian Sauce

This filling vegetarian dish is perfect for an inexpensive and quick lunch.

Serves 4

INGREDIENTS

5 tbsp olive oil
3 garlic cloves, crushed
2 fresh red chillies, chopped

1 green chilli, chopped
200 ml/7 fl oz/^{7}/$_8$ cup Italian Red
Wine Sauce (see Cook's Tip)

400 g/14 oz/3^1/$_2$ cups dried rotelle
salt and pepper
warm Italian bread, to serve

1 Make the Italian Red Wine Sauce (see Cook's Tip, right).

2 Heat 4 tbsp of the oil in a saucepan. Add the garlic and chillies and fry for 3 minutes.

3 Stir in the Italian Red Wine Sauce (see Cook's Tip, right), season with salt and pepper to taste, and simmer gently over a low heat for 20 minutes.

4 Bring a large saucepan of lightly salted water to the boil. Add the rotelle and the remaining oil and cook for 8 minutes, until just tender, but still firm to the bite. Drain the pasta.

5 Toss the rotelle in the spicy sauce, transfer to a warm serving dish and serve with warm Italian bread.

COOK'S TIP

Take care when using fresh chillies as they can burn your skin. Handle them as little as possible – wear rubber gloves if necessary. Always wash your hands thoroughly afterwards and don't touch your face or eyes before you have washed your hands. Remove chilli seeds before chopping the chillies, as they are the hottest part, and shouldn't be allowed to slip into the food.

COOK'S TIP

To make Italian Red Wine Sauce, first make a demi-glace sauce by combining 150 ml/^{1}/$_4$ pint/^{5}/$_8$ cup each Brown Stock and Espagnole Sauce, cook for 10 minutes and strain. Meanwhile, combine 125 ml/4 fl oz/^{1}/$_2$ cup red wine, 2 tbsp red wine vinegar, 4 tbsp chopped shallots, 1 bay leaf and 1 thyme sprig in a small saucepan. Bring to the boil and reduce by about three-quarters. Add the demi-glace sauce and simmer for 20 minutes. Season with pepper and strain.

Creamy Pasta & Broccoli

This colourful dish provides a mouth-watering contrast in the crisp 'al dente' texture of the broccoli and the creamy cheese sauce.

Serves 4

INGREDIENTS

60 g/2 oz/4 tbsp butter
1 large onion, finely chopped
450 g/1 lb dried ribbon pasta
460 g/1 lb broccoli, broken into
  florets (flowerets)

150 ml/^{1}/4 pint/^{5}/8 cup boiling
  vegetable stock
1 tbsp plain (all purpose) flour
150 ml/^{1}/4 pint/^{5}/8 cup single
  (light) cream

60 g/2 oz/^{1}/2 cup grated
  mozzarella cheese
freshly grated nutmeg
salt and white pepper
fresh apple slices, to garnish

1 Melt half of the butter in a large saucepan over a medium heat. Add the onion and fry for 4 minutes.

2 Add the broccoli and pasta to the pan and cook, stirring constantly, for 2 minutes. Add the vegetable stock, bring back to the boil and simmer for a further 12 minutes. Season well with salt and white pepper.

3 Meanwhile, melt the remaining butter in a saucepan over a medium heat.

Sprinkle over the flour and cook, stirring constantly, for 2 minutes. Gradually stir in the cream and bring to simmering point, but do not boil. Add the grated cheese and season with salt and a little freshly grated nutmeg.

4 Drain the pasta and broccoli mixture and pour over the cheese sauce. Cook, stirring occasionally, for about 2 minutes. Transfer the pasta and broccoli mixture to a warm, large, deep serving dish and serve garnished with slices of fresh apple.

VARIATION

This dish would also be delicious and look just as colourful made with Cape broccoli, which is actually a purple variety of cauliflower and not broccoli at all.

Three Cheese Bake

Serve this dish while the cheese is still hot and melted, as cooked cheese turns very rubbery if it is allowed to cool down.

Serves 4

INGREDIENTS

butter, for greasing
400 g/14 oz dried penne
1 tbsp olive oil
2 eggs, beaten

350 g/12 oz/1$\frac{1}{2}$ cups ricotta cheese
4 fresh basil sprigs
100 g/3$\frac{1}{2}$ oz/1 cup grated
  mozzarella or halloumi cheese

4 tbsp freshly grated
  Parmesan cheese
salt and black pepper
fresh basil leaves (optional), to garnish

1 Lightly grease an ovenproof dish with butter.

2 Bring a large pan of lightly salted water to the boil. Add the penne and olive oil and cook until just tender, but still firm to the bite. Drain the pasta, set aside and keep warm.

3 Beat the eggs into the ricotta cheese and season to taste with salt and pepper.

4 Spoon half the penne into the base of the dish and cover with half the ricotta cheese mixture.

5 Arrange half of the basil leaves on top of the ricotta mixture. Sprinkle over the mozzarella or halloumi cheese and top with the remaining basil leaves. Cover with the remaining penne and then spoon over the remaining ricotta cheese mixture. Sprinkle over the grated Parmesan cheese.

6 Bake in a preheated oven at 190°C/375°F/Gas 5 for 30–40 minutes, until golden brown and the cheese topping is hot and bubbling. Garnish with fresh basil leaves, if liked, and serve hot.

VARIATION

Try substituting smoked Bavarian cheese for the mozzarella or halloumi and grated Cheddar cheese for the Parmesan, for a slightly different but just as delicious flavour.

Vegetable Lasagne

This colourful and tasty lasagne, with layers of vegetables in tomato sauce and
aubergines (eggplants), all topped with a rich cheese sauce is simply delicious.

Serves 4

INGREDIENTS

1 aubergine (eggplant), sliced
3 tbsp olive oil
2 garlic cloves, crushed
1 red onion, halved and sliced
1 green (bell) pepper, diced
1 red (bell) pepper, diced
1 yellow (bell) pepper, diced
225 g/8 oz mixed mushrooms, sliced
2 celery sticks, sliced
1 courgette (zucchini), diced

$1/2$ tsp chilli powder
$1/2$ tsp ground cumin
2 tomatoes, chopped
300 ml/$1/2$ pint/$1\,1/4$ cups passata
  (sieved tomatoes)
2 tbsp chopped basil
8 no pre-cook lasagne verdi sheets
salt and pepper

CHEESE SAUCE:
2 tbsp butter or vegetarian margarine
1 tbsp flour
150 ml/$1/4$ pint/$2/3$ cup vegetable
  stock
300 ml/$1/2$ pint/$1\,1/4$ cups milk
75 g/$2\,3/4$ oz/$3/4$ cup vegetarian
  Cheddar, grated
1 tsp Dijon mustard
1 tbsp chopped basil
1 egg, beaten

1 Place the aubergine (eggplant) slices in a colander, sprinkle with salt and leave for 20 minutes. Rinse under cold water, drain and reserve. Heat the oil in a pan and sauté the garlic and onion for 1–2 minutes. Add the (bell) peppers, mushrooms, celery and courgette (zucchini) and cook for 3–4 minutes, stirring. Stir in the spices and cook for 1 minute. Mix the tomatoes, passata (sieved tomatoes) and basil together and season well.

2 For the sauce, melt the butter in a pan, add the flour and cook for 1 minute. Remove from the heat and stir in the stock and milk. Return to the heat and add half of the cheese and the mustard. Boil, stirring, until thickened. Stir in the basil and season. Remove from the heat and stir in the egg. Place half of the lasagne sheets in an ovenproof dish. Top with half of the vegetables, then half of the tomato sauce. Cover with half the aubergines (eggplants). Repeat and spoon the cheese sauce on top. Sprinkle with cheese and cook in a preheated oven, 180°C/350°F/ Gas 4, for 40 minutes.

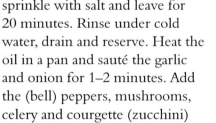

Baked Cheese & Tomato Macaroni

This is a really simple, family dish which is easy to prepare and cook. Serve with a salad.

Serves 4

Delicious!
Very easy to make

INGREDIENTS

225 g/8 oz/2 cups elbow macaroni
175 g/6 oz/1½ cups grated
  vegetarian cheese
100 g/3½ oz/1 cup grated Parmesan
  cheese
4 tbsp fresh white breadcrumbs

1 tbsp chopped basil
1 tbsp butter or margarine

TOMATO SAUCE:
1 tbsp olive oil
1 shallot, finely chopped

2 garlic cloves, crushed
550g 450 g/1 lb canned chopped tomatoes
1 tbsp chopped basil
salt and pepper

1 To make the tomato sauce, heat the oil in a saucepan and sauté the shallots and garlic for 1 minute. Add the tomatoes, basil, salt and pepper to taste and cook over a medium heat, stirring, for 10 minutes.

2 Meanwhile, cook the macaroni in a pan of boiling salted water for 8 minutes or until just undercooked. Drain.

3 Mix both of the cheeses together.

4 Grease a deep, ovenproof dish. Spoon a third of the tomato sauce into the base of the dish, top with a third of the macaroni and then a third of the cheeses. Season with salt and pepper. Repeat the layers twice.

5 Combine the breadcrumbs and basil and sprinkle over the top. Dot with the butter or margarine and cook in a preheated oven, 190°C/375°F/Gas Mark 5, for 25 minutes or until the dish is golden brown and bubbling. Serve.

COOK'S TIP

Use other pasta shapes, such as penne, if you have them to hand, instead of the macaroni.

Vegetable Cannelloni

This dish is made with prepared cannelloni tubes,
but may also be made by rolling ready-bought lasagne sheets.

Serves 4

INGREDIENTS

1 aubergine (eggplant)
125 ml/4 fl oz/^{1}/$_2$ cup olive oil
225 g/8 oz spinach
2 garlic cloves, crushed
1 tsp ground cumin
75 g/2^3/$_4$ oz/1 cup mushrooms,
   chopped

12 cannelloni tubes
salt and pepper

TOMATO SAUCE:
1 tbsp olive oil
1 onion, chopped
2 garlic cloves, crushed

2 x 400 g/14 oz cans chopped
   tomatoes
1 tsp caster (superfine) sugar
2 tbsp chopped basil
50 g/1^3/$_4$ oz/^{1}/$_2$ cup Mozzarella,
   sliced

1 Cut the aubergine (eggplant) into small dice.

2 Heat the oil in a frying pan (skillet) and cook the aubergine (eggplant) for 2–3 minutes.

3 Add the spinach, garlic, cumin and mushrooms. Season and cook for 2–3 minutes, stirring. Spoon the mixture into the cannelloni tubes and place in an ovenproof dish in a single layer.

4 To make the sauce, heat the olive oil in a saucepan and sauté the onion and garlic for 1 minute. Add the tomatoes, caster (superfine) sugar and chopped basil and bring to the boil. Reduce the heat and simmer for about 5 minutes. Pour the sauce over the cannelloni tubes.

5 Arrange the sliced Mozzarella on top of the sauce and cook in a preheated oven, 190°C/375°F/ Gas Mark 5, for 30 minutes or until the cheese is bubbling and golden brown. Serve immediately.

COOK'S TIP

You can prepare the tomato sauce in advance and store it in the refrigerator for up to 24 hours.

Tagliatelle with Courgette (Zucchini) Sauce

This is a really fresh tasting dish which is ideal with
a crisp white wine and some crusty bread.

Serves 4

INGREDIENTS

650 g/1 lb 7 oz courgettes (zucchini)
6 tbsp olive oil
3 garlic cloves, crushed
3 tbsp chopped basil
2 red chillies, sliced

juice of 1 large lemon
5 tbsp single (light) cream
4 tbsp grated Parmesan cheese
225 g/8 oz tagliatelle
salt and pepper

1 Using a vegetable peeler, slice the courgettes (zucchini) into thin ribbons.

2 Heat the oil in a frying pan (skillet) and sauté the garlic for 30 seconds.

3 Add the courgettes (zucchini) and cook over a gentle heat, stirring, for 5–7 minutes.

4 Stir in the basil, chillies, lemon juice, single (light) cream and grated Parmesan cheese and season with salt and pepper to taste.

5 Meanwhile, cook the tagliatelle in a large pan of lightly salted boiling water for 10 minutes until 'al dente'. Drain the pasta thoroughly and put in a warm serving bowl.

6 Pile the courgette (zucchini) mixture on top of the pasta. Serve immediately.

VARIATION

Lime juice and
zest could be used instead of the
lemon
as an alternative.

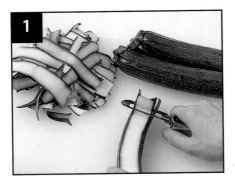

Olive, (Bell) Pepper & Cherry Tomato Pasta

The sweet cherry tomatoes in this recipe add colour and flavour and are complemented by the black olives and (bell) peppers.

Serves 4

INGREDIENTS

225 g/8 oz/2 cups penne
2 tbsp olive oil
2 tbsp butter
2 garlic cloves, crushed
1 green (bell) pepper, thinly sliced

1 yellow (bell) pepper, thinly sliced
16 cherry tomatoes, halved
1 tbsp chopped oregano
125 ml/4 fl oz/$\frac{1}{2}$ cup dry white wine
2 tbsp quartered, pitted black olives

75 g/2$\frac{3}{4}$ oz rocket
salt and pepper
fresh oregano sprigs, to garnish

1 Cook the pasta in a saucepan of boiling salted water for 8–10 minutes or until 'al dente'. Drain thoroughly.

2 Heat the oil and butter in a pan until the butter melts. Sauté the garlic for 30 seconds. Add the (bell) peppers and cook for 3–4 minutes, stirring.

3 Stir in the cherry tomatoes, oregano, wine and olives and cook for 3–4 minutes. Season well with salt and pepper and stir in the rocket until just wilted.

4 Transfer the pasta to a serving dish, spoon over the sauce and mix well. Garnish and serve.

VARIATION

If rocket is unavailable, spinach makes a good substitute. Follow the same cooking instructions as for rocket.

COOK'S TIP

Ensure that the saucepan is large enough to prevent the pasta from sticking together during cooking.

Spinach & Pine Kernel (Nut) Pasta

Use any pasta shapes that you have for this recipe,
the tricolore pasta being visually the best to use.

Serves 4

INGREDIENTS

225 g/8 oz pasta shapes or spaghetti
125 ml/4 fl oz/$^1/_2$ cup olive oil
2 garlic cloves, crushed
1 onion, quartered and sliced
3 large flat mushrooms, sliced

225 g/8 oz spinach
2 tbsp pine kernels (nuts)
85 ml/3 fl oz/6 tbsp dry white wine
salt and pepper
Parmesan shavings, to garnish

1 Cook the pasta in a saucepan of boiling salted water for 8–10 minutes or until 'al dente'. Drain well.

2 Meanwhile, heat the oil in a large saucepan and sauté the garlic and onion for 1 minute.

3 Add the sliced mushrooms and cook for 2 minutes, stirring occasionally.

4 Add the spinach and cook for 4–5 minutes or until the spinach has wilted.

5 Stir in the pine kernels (nuts) and wine, season well and cook for 1 minute.

6 Transfer the pasta to a warm serving bowl and toss the sauce into it, mixing well. Garnish with shavings of Parmesan cheese and serve.

COOK'S TIP

'Al dente' means that the pasta
should be tender but still
have a bite to it.

COOK'S TIP

Freshly grate a little nutmeg over
the dish for extra flavour as it is
particularly good with spinach.

Fettuccine all'Alfredo

This simple, traditional dish can be made with any long pasta,
but is especially good with flat noodles, such as fettuccine or tagliatelle.

Serves 4

INGREDIENTS

25 g/1 oz/2 tbsp butter
200 ml/7 fl oz/⁷⁄₈ cup double (heavy) cream
460 g/1 lb fresh fettuccine

1 tbsp olive oil
90 g/3 oz/1 cup freshly grated Parmesan cheese, plus extra to serve

pinch of freshly grated nutmeg
salt and pepper
fresh parsley sprigs, to garnish

1 Put the butter and 150 ml/ ¼ pint/⁵⁄₈ cup of the cream in a large saucepan and bring the mixture to the boil over a medium heat. Reduce the heat and then simmer gently for about 1½ minutes, or until slightly thickened.

2 Meanwhile, bring a large pan of lightly salted water to the boil. Add the fettuccine and olive oil and cook for 2–3 minutes, until tender but still firm to the bite. Drain the fettuccine thoroughly and then pour over the cream sauce.

3 Toss the fettuccine in the sauce over a low heat until thoroughly coated.

4 Add the remaining cream, the Parmesan cheese and nutmeg to the fettuccine mixture and season to taste with salt and pepper. Toss thoroughly to coat while gently heating through.

5 Transfer the fettucine mixture to a warm serving plate and garnish with the fresh sprig of parsley. Serve immediately, handing extra grated Parmesan cheese separately.

VARIATION

This classic Roman dish is often served with the addition of strips of ham and fresh peas. Add 225 g/ 8 oz/2 cups shelled cooked peas and 175 g/6 oz ham strips with the Parmesan cheese in step 4.

Pasta & Bean Casserole

A satisfying winter dish, pasta and bean casserole with a crunchy topping is a slow-cooked, one-pot meal.

Serves 6

INGREDIENTS

225 g/8 oz/1¼ cups dried haricot (navy) beans, soaked overnight and drained
225 g/8 oz dried penne
6 tbsp olive oil
850 ml/1½ pints /3½ cups vegetable stock
2 large onions, sliced

2 garlic cloves, chopped
2 bay leaves
1 tsp dried oregano
1 tsp dried thyme
5 tbsp red wine
2 tbsp tomato purée (paste)
2 celery sticks (stalks), sliced
1 fennel bulb, sliced

115 g/4 oz/1⅝ cups sliced mushrooms
250 g/8 oz tomatoes, sliced
1 tsp dark muscovado sugar
4 tbsp dry white breadcrumbs
salt and pepper
salad leaves (greens) and crusty bread, to serve

1 Put the haricot (navy) beans in a large saucepan and add sufficient cold water to cover. Bring to the boil and continue to boil vigorously for 20 minutes. Drain, set aside and keep warm.

2 Bring a large saucepan of lightly salted water to the boil. Add the penne and 1 tbsp of the olive oil and cook for about 3 minutes. Drain the pasta, set aside and keep warm.

3 Put the beans in a large, flameproof casserole. Add the vegetable stock and stir in the remaining olive oil, the onions, garlic, bay leaves, oregano, thyme, wine and tomato purée (paste). Bring to the boil, then cover and cook in a preheated oven at 180°C/350°F/Gas 4 for 2 hours.

4 Add the penne, celery, fennel, mushrooms and tomatoes to the casserole and season to taste with salt and pepper. Stir in the muscovado sugar and sprinkle over the breadcrumbs. Cover the dish and cook in the oven for 1 further hour.

5 Serve hot with salad leaves (greens) and crusty bread.

Green Tagliatelle with Garlic

A rich pasta dish for garlic lovers everywhere.
It is quick and easy to prepare and full of flavour.

Serves 4

INGREDIENTS

2 tbsp walnut oil
1 bunch spring onions
   (scallions), sliced
2 garlic cloves, thinly sliced
250 g/8 oz/3¹/₄ cups sliced
   mushrooms
450 g/1 lb fresh green and white
   tagliatelle

1 tbsp olive oil
225 g/8 oz frozen spinach, thawed
   and drained
115 g/4 oz/¹/₂ cup full-fat soft
   cheese with garlic and herbs
4 tbsp single (light) cream
60 g/2 oz/¹/₂ cup chopped, unsalted
   pistachio nuts

salt and pepper

TO GARNISH:
2 tbsp shredded fresh basil
fresh basil sprigs
Italian bread, to serve

1 Heat the walnut oil in a large frying pan (skillet). Add the spring onions (scallions) and garlic and fry for 1 minute, until just softened.

2 Add the mushrooms to the pan, stir well, cover and cook over a low heat for about 5 minutes, until softened.

3 Meanwhile, bring a large saucepan of lightly salted water to the boil. Add the tagliatelle and olive oil and cook for 3–5 minutes, until tender but still firm to the bite. Drain the tagliatelle thoroughly and return to the saucepan.

4 Add the spinach to the frying pan (skillet) and heat through for 1–2 minutes. Add the cheese to the pan and allow to melt slightly. Stir in the cream and continue to cook, without allowing the mixture to come to the boil, until warmed through.

5 Pour the sauce over the pasta, season to taste with salt and black pepper and mix well. Heat through gently, stirring constantly, for 2–3 minutes.

6 Transfer the pasta to a serving dish and sprinkle with the pistachio nuts and shredded basil. Garnish with the basil sprigs and serve immediately with the Italian bread of your choice.

Spaghetti Olio e Aglio

*This easy and satisfying Roman dish originated as a cheap meal for poor people,
but has now become a favourite in restaurants and trattorias.*

Serves 4

INGREDIENTS

125 ml/4 fl oz/$^{1}/_{2}$ cup olive oil
3 garlic cloves, crushed

460 g/1 lb fresh spaghetti

3 tbsp roughly chopped fresh parsley
salt and pepper

1 Reserve 1 tbsp of the olive oil and heat the remainder in a medium saucepan. Add the garlic and a pinch of salt and cook over a low heat, stirring constantly, until golden brown, then remove the pan from the heat. Do not allow the garlic to burn as it will taint its flavour. (If it does burn, you will have to start all over again!).

2 Meanwhile, bring a large saucepan of lightly salted water to the boil. Add the spaghetti and remaining olive oil and cook for 2–3 minutes, until tender, but still firm to the bite. Drain the spaghetti thoroughly and return to the pan.

3 Add the oil and garlic mixture to the spaghetti and toss to coat thoroughly. Season with pepper, add the chopped fresh parsley and toss to coat again.

4 Transfer the spaghetti to a warm serving dish and serve immediately.

COOK'S TIP

Oils produced by different countries, mainly Italy, Spain and Greece, have their own characteristic flavours. Some produce an oil which has a hot, peppery taste while others have a 'green' flavour.

COOK'S TIP

It is worth buying the best-quality olive oil for dishes such as this one which makes a feature of its flavour, and for salad dressings in addition. Extra virgin oil is produced from the first pressing and has the lowest acidity. It is more expensive than other types of olive oil, but has the finest flavour. Virgin olive oil is slightly more acid, but is also well flavoured. Oil simply labelled pure has usually been heat-treated and refined by mechanical means and, consequently, lacks character and flavour.

Patriotic Pasta

*The ingredients of this dish have the same
bright colours as the Italian flag – hence its name.*

Serves 4

INGREDIENTS

460 g/1 lb/4 cups dried farfalle
4 tbsp olive oil

460 g/1 lb cherry tomatoes
90 g/3 oz rocket (arugula)

salt and pepper
Pecorino cheese, to garnish

1 Bring a large saucepan of lightly salted water to the boil. Add the farfalle and 1 tbsp of the olive oil and cook until tender, but still firm to the bite. Drain the farfalle thoroughly and return to the pan.

2 Cut the cherry tomatoes in half and trim the rocket (arugula).

3 Heat the remaining olive oil in a large saucepan. Add the tomatoes and cook for 1 minute. Add the farfalle and the rocket (arugula) and stir gently to mix. Heat through and season to taste with salt and black pepper.

4 Meanwhile, using a vegetable peeler, shave thin slices of Pecorino cheese.

5 Transfer the farfalle and vegetables to a warm serving dish. Garnish with the Pecorino cheese shavings and serve immediately.

COOK'S TIP

Pecorino cheese is a hard sheep's milk cheese which resembles Parmesan and is often used for grating over a variety of dishes. It has a sharp flavour and is only used in small quantities.

COOK'S TIP

Rocket (arugula) is a small plant with irregular-shaped leaves rather like those of turnip tops (greens). The flavour is distinctively peppery and slightly reminiscent of radish. It has always been popular in Italy, both in salads and for serving with pasta and has recently enjoyed a revival in Britain and the United States, where it has now become very fashionable.

Mediterranean Spaghetti

Delicious Mediterranean vegetables, cooked in rich tomato sauce,
make an ideal topping for nutty wholemeal (whole-wheat) pasta.

Serves 4

INGREDIENTS

2 tbsp olive oil
1 large, red onion, chopped
2 garlic cloves, crushed
1 tbsp lemon juice
4 baby aubergines (eggplant),
    quartered

600 ml/1 pint/2$\frac{1}{2}$ cups passata
    (sieved tomatoes)
2 tsp caster (superfine) sugar
2 tbsp tomato purée (paste)
400 g/14 oz can artichoke hearts,
    drained and halved

115 g/4 oz/1 cup stoned (pitted)
    black olives
350 g/12 oz dried spaghetti
25 g/1 oz/2 tbsp butter
salt and pepper
fresh basil sprigs, to garnish
olive bread, to serve

1 Heat 1 tbsp of the olive oil in a large frying pan (skillet). Add the onion, garlic, lemon juice and aubergines (eggplant) and cook over a low heat for 4–5 minutes, until the onion and aubergines (eggplant) are lightly golden brown.

2 Pour in the passata (sieved tomatoes), season to taste with salt and black pepper and stir in the caster (superfine) sugar and tomato purée (paste). Bring to the boil, lower the heat and then simmer, stirring occasionally, for 20 minutes.

3 Gently stir in the artichoke hearts and black olives and cook for 5 minutes.

4 Meanwhile, bring a large saucepan of lightly salted water to the boil. Add the spaghetti and the remaining oil and cook for 7–8 minutes, until tender but still firm to the bite.

5 Drain the spaghetti thoroughly and toss with the butter. Transfer the spaghetti to a large serving dish.

6 Pour the vegetable sauce over the spaghetti, garnish with the sprigs of fresh basil and serve immediately with olive bread.

Spinach & Wild Mushroom Lasagne

This is one of the tastiest vegetarian dishes. Always check the seasoning of vegetables, as it is most important. You can always add a little more seasoning to a recipe, but you cannot take it out once it has been added.

Serves 4

INGREDIENTS

115 g/4 oz/8 tbsp butter, plus extra
  for greasing
2 garlic cloves, finely chopped
115 g/4 oz shallots
225 g/8 oz wild mushrooms, such as
  chanterelles

450 g/1 lb spinach, cooked, drained
  and finely chopped
225 g/8 oz/2 cups grated
  Cheddar cheese
$1/4$ tsp freshly grated nutmeg
1 tsp chopped fresh basil

60 g/2 oz plain (all purpose) flour
600 ml/1 pint/$2^1/_2$ cups hot milk
60 g/2 oz/$^2/_3$ cup grated Cheshire
  cheese
salt and pepper
8 sheets pre-cooked lasagne

1 Lightly grease an ovenproof dish with a little butter.

2 Melt 60 g/2 oz/4 tbsp of the butter in a saucepan. Add the garlic, shallots and wild mushrooms and fry over a low heat for 3 minutes. Stir in the spinach, Cheddar cheese, nutmeg and basil. Season well with salt and black pepper and set aside.

3 Melt the remaining butter in another saucepan over a low heat. Add the flour and cook, stirring constantly, for 1 minute. Gradually stir in the hot milk, whisking constantly until smooth. Stir in 25 g/1 oz/$1/4$ cup of the Cheshire cheese and season to taste with salt and black pepper.

4 Spread half of the mushroom and spinach mixture over the base of the prepared dish. Cover with a layer of lasagne and then with half of the cheese sauce. Repeat the process and sprinkle over the remaining Cheshire cheese. Bake in a preheated oven at 200°C/400°F/Gas 6 for 30 minutes, until golden brown.

VARIATION

You could substitute 4 (bell) peppers for the spinach. Roast in a preheated oven at 200°C/400°F/ Gas Mark 6 for 20 minutes. Rub off the skins under cold water, deseed and chop before using.

Vermicelli Flan

*Lightly cooked vermicelli is pressed into a flan ring
and baked with a creamy mushroom filling.*

Serves 4

INGREDIENTS

75 g/3 oz/6 tbsp butter, plus extra,
   for greasing
225 g/8 oz dried vermicelli or
   spaghetti
1 tbsp olive oil
1 onion, chopped

140 g/5 oz button mushrooms
1 green (bell) pepper, cored, seeded
   and sliced into thin rings
150 ml/$\frac{1}{4}$ pint/$\frac{5}{8}$ cup milk
3 eggs, lightly beaten
2 tbsp double (heavy) cream

1 tsp dried oregano
freshly grated nutmeg
1 tbsp freshly grated Parmesan
   cheese
salt and pepper
tomato and basil salad, to serve

1 Generously grease a 20 cm/
8 inch loose-based flan tin
(pan) with butter.

2 Bring a large pan of lightly
salted water to the boil. Add
the vermicelli and olive oil and
cook until tender, but still firm to
the bite. Drain, return to the pan,
add 25 g/1 oz/2 tbsp of the butter
and shake the pan to coat the pasta.

3 Press the pasta on to the base
and around the sides of the
flan tin (pan) to make a flan case.

4 Melt the remaining butter in a
frying pan (skillet) over a
medium heat. Add the onion and
fry until it is translucent. Remove
the onion from the pan with a
slotted spoon and spread it evenly
over the base of the flan case.

5 Add the mushrooms and
(bell) pepper rings to the
frying pan (skillet) and cook,
stirring and turning constantly, for
2–3 minutes. Remove from the
pan with a slotted spoon and
arrange them in the flan case.

6 Beat together the milk, eggs
and cream, stir in the oregano
and season to taste with nutmeg
and black pepper. Carefully pour
the mixture over the vegetables
and sprinkle over the cheese.

7 Bake the flan in a preheated
oven at 180°C/350°F/Gas 4
for 40–45 minutes, until the filling
has set.

8 Slide the flan out of the tin
(pan) and serve warm with a
tomato and basil salad.

This is a Parragon Book
First published in 2003

Parragon
Queen Street House
4 Queen Street, Bath, BA1 1HE, UK

ISBN: 1-40540-837-5

Printed in China

NOTE

This book uses imperial and metric measurements. Follow the same units of measurement throughout; do not mix imperial and metric. All spoon measurements are level; teaspoons are assumed to be 5 ml and tablespoons are assumed to be 15 ml. Unless otherwise stated, milk is assumed to be whole milk, eggs and individual vegetables such as potatoes are medium, and pepper is freshly ground black pepper.

The times given for each recipe are an approximate guide only because the preparation times may differ according to the techniques used by different people and the cooking times may vary as a result of the type of oven used.

Recipes using raw or very lightly cooked eggs should be avoided by infants, the elderly, pregnant women, convalescents and anyone suffering from an illness.